The Mary Julia Paintings of Joan Brown

The Mary Julia Paintings of Joan Brown

William Benton

Pressed Wafer | Brooklyn NY

Books by William Benton

POETRY
The Bell Poems
Eye La View
L'après-midi d'un faune
Normal Meanings
Marmalade
Birds

PROSE
Exchanging Hats: Elizabeth Bishop Paintings
Deaf Elephants (Children's Book)
Madly (novel)

EDITOR
Gods of Tin: The Flying Years by James Salter
"A Quatrain for Sleeping Beauty" by Stéphane Mallarmé

PRESSED WAFER
375 Parkside Avenue, Brooklyn NY 11226
www.pressedwafer.com

My Mary Julia

ELAINE WAS SLENDER with wide-set dark eyes and brown straight hair. We were living in Key West when we separated. Our daughter, who was seven at the time, waved tearfully from the window of the bus as it pulled out. Our son, a year and a half younger, turned his face away. We had come to an end—of the physical continent and of our marriage. I stayed in Key West for a few weeks, until I raised enough money to leave.

Two years earlier, we'd sold our house in Portland, Oregon, where I was working as the dean of an art school, to chase down the happiness of a new life in Mexico. We went first to Guadalajara and then to Puerto Vallarta. The children got sick from drinking the water, and Elaine, convinced that Mexico had been a mistake, took them to Hawaii to recover. An old boyfriend of hers lived in Honolulu. Years before, they had hiked the Na Pali Coast together. We treated this less as a separation than a break from each other. A month later we met up in California and, with money running low, began to look for a place to live. We ended up renting a house in Santa Barbara, where we stayed for almost a year. Elaine was unhappy in ways elusive to both of us. She talked about ending the marriage, but at the same time turned to me for solace in the face of its loss. An opaque complexity (if she was its architect, she was also its most innocent victim) left us clinging helplessly to each other. Finally, Elaine decided it was over and asked me to move out. Through a friend I got an adjunct teaching position at the University of Cincinnati. Elaine and the children saw me off at the airport.

A month later she had changed her mind and drove across the country with the children to Cincinnati. In the euphoric moments of reconciliation, Elaine proposed that we move to Key West and, beside a warm ocean, put our marriage back together. I quit my teaching job in mid-semester. We spent the winter and spring in Key West. Instead of reviving our marriage, the simple days of sun and sea only further exposed its difficulties. We drank a lot, living with a sense of suspension and displacement. The day she left, we walked to the bus station together. It was late afternoon, with the asphalt

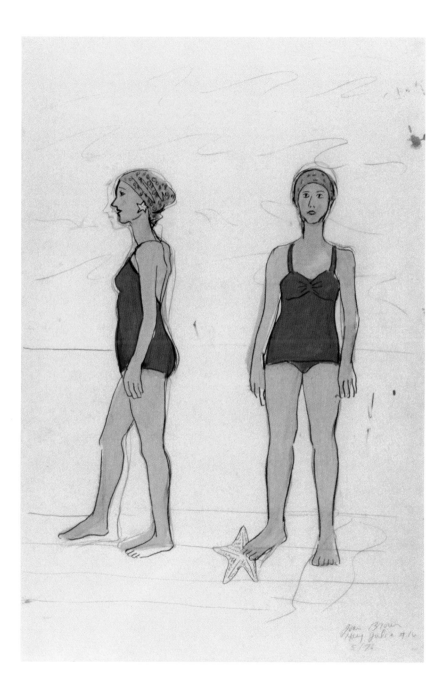

of the streets still soft in the blazing heat. That night there was a full moon. Somewhere along the highway going north, she must have seen it too. It was like a little a parable of our lives. The one that followed her away stayed. The one that stayed followed her away.

I WENT from Key West to Santa Fe. It was on the American circuit of misfits and failures, but also was a place known for its art community. I was thirty-six, broke, a poet with four published books and an art-related background. There were dozens and dozens of galleries scattered through the town and up its legendary Canyon Road. I contacted the *New Mexican*, the local newspaper, about writing art reviews. They had a regular critic but hired me to do a one-time piece based on my first impressions of the Santa Fe art scene. After the article appeared, the owner of one of the galleries I'd visited, a dapper, silver-haired hippie who drove a Bentley around town and spoke with a pretentious-sounding, upper-crust accent, offered me a job.

Parting, like mating, has its own choreography. As soon as I was settled
in Santa Fe, Elaine had a change of heart. She and the children flew out
from Canada, where she'd been staying with her parents. We lived together
again for a while, but this time when things failed to work out Elaine rented
a place of her own and enrolled the children in school. The separation,
without geographic distance, was, unlike the others, internalized. It involved
a permanence that had taken hold, almost without our knowledge. My rages
against it, subverted in Elaine's silences to a specious cause of our defeat, fell
away like a broken wheel.

Later that year, with a friend of mine, I opened the Clarke-Benton Gallery
in downtown Santa Fe—not far from where Elaine was living. Joan Brown's
Mary Julia Series was one of the gallery's early shows. Roy De Forest, whose
manic gang of dogs had been our first exhibition, put me in touch with Joan.
She was an artist I admired, but had never met. When I called her in San
Francisco, she said she had a group of acrylic paintings on paper that were

ready to go and generously offered to fly out with the work for the opening. In Joan's self-portraits she was green-eyed and good-looking. The next time we talked, about framing preparations and the dimensions of the gallery space, an element of friendly flirtation was present on both sides of the conversation. She was a long-distance swimmer. I'd seen reproductions of several large canvases documenting her Alcatraz swim.

"What strokes do you use?"

"Only the crawl," she said.

"For that distance?"

"There's a knack to it. I'll teach you when I get there, if they have a pool where I'm staying."

We arranged that I would meet her at the Albuquerque airport.

"How will I know you?" she asked.

"I'll be the one in the bathing suit."

She didn't laugh. In a cool, unfazed voice, she said, "Oh, good."

THE NIGHT JOAN ARRIVED we unpacked the work in the gallery. The pictures, perhaps twenty in all, were vertical compositions of a single female figure in a variety of poses and costumes. The paint, in strong colors, was handled with deft, in-and-out insouciance. Matisse had been a major influence on the Bay Area Figurative School. There were sacerdotal borrowings in the work of David Park, Elmer Bischoff, and Richard Diebenkorn. Joan, a few years younger than they, simply appropriated what she needed from Matisse. In her case it was an unceremonious act that in its very attitude expressed originality. The paintings she'd brought, done in a series, made an almost overt reference to *Interior with Egyptian Curtain*, a late Matisse painting from the period in Vence. In Matisse's picture, a pear and a bowl of fruit sit on a narrow table in front of a window that looks out at a shimmering, sun-bright palm. On one side of the window a decorative curtain hangs down. Painted when Matisse was seventy-nine and ill, its intense summery exterior, set against the black of the room and the black

ground of the curtain, seems to contain, like a hymn to life, a knowledge of what the closed curtain would mean.

In the *Mary Julia Series* the table and bowl of fruit are gone, replaced by the willowy figure of a young woman in much the same setting. Whether or not Joan arrived at these pictures with *Interior with Egyptian Curtain* in mind, the thought of it fit in with the strength and confidence of her work.

We went through the paintings together. In each, scenes and seasons change in the window behind the figure, along with the colors of the room and the curtains' designs, but the same motif, with a few exceptions, recurs throughout the series. I watched the pictures flash by. Elegant, in a powder-blue dress, matching heels, and a navy feather boa dangling down past her waist, Mary Julia stands in front of a pink wall. Out the window, black buildings in the San Francisco skyline are lit with myriad dots of yellow, against a deep cobalt sky. In another, thin winter branches thread the light blue sky of the window, with black curtains on each side patterned in red-

and-yellow, zigzag diamond shapes. (In the same picture, Mary Julia, with her hands perched on the top of a wide-brimmed hat, creates a rhyming diamond shape with her arms.) In another, the figure stands on a brilliant, red carpet with a symmetrical, green-and-yellow floral design, which is painted as a flat plane without perspective. Dressed in heels and an elegant black bodysuit, she holds a gray cape behind her like a matador, prepared to take on the night. In what we can imagine as a large window that exceeds the frame of the picture, a seductive dusk-blue fills the background, with the silhouette of Alcatraz and the Bay Bridge in the distance.

The pictures were intimate, witty, sexy, glamorous—evocative of the iconic diversity of a woman's life. Yet, for me, by far the most astonishing thing about them was that the figure in the paintings *looked exactly like Elaine*. The physical resemblance was extraordinary—it was Elaine's body, her face, her hair—but also her spirit, the style of wearing hats and vintage clothing with the ease and natural flair of a performance. At the opening, which Elaine

attended, a number of people commented on how much the woman in the pictures resembled her. "I've been painting you," Joan said, when I introduced them.

THE MARY JULIA SERIES had its start in drawing sessions held at Manuel Neri's studio, in San Francisco, where Joan and a few other artists regularly got together. Neri, an acclaimed sculptor, was Joan's ex-husband from a decade earlier and the father of their son Noel. They'd remained close friends and competitors. Mary Julia Klimenko, a young poet and Neri's girlfriend, became the group's model. She didn't look anything like Joan, who was elfin and fair, but took on in the Mary Julia Series the role of her alter ego. Like the Hollywood actresses Joan had drawn as a teenager, Mary Julia played the part of "Joan Brown" in the brief narratives that shifted from picture to picture. This doubling and distancing gave to the image itself, at least in my mind, a subtle autonomy; it was freer to assume a coincident likeness.

I spent the next month surrounded in the gallery by vivid images of my wife. I went home each night to my apartment haunted by the show. I loved the paintings. And I loved Elaine.

ELAINE HAD MOVED from rural Canada and a quiet middle-class upbringing to New York City when she was eighteen or nineteen. Her life was centered in the East Village. She worked as a waitress at the Ninth Circle, studied photography for a while. Eventually, she married a man twelve years older than she. They had a son. From the start, Elaine was perhaps less prepared emotionally for New York than most young women coming to the city on their own. It wasn't just lack of experience or Canadian naiveté. She possessed an innate, optimistic openness that met the world more than halfway. Her essential nature was vibrant, funny, trusting; yet beneath it, like a missing dimension, there was little or no counterpart in her makeup to absorb the bad things that happen to people. In the invidious laws that

operate at this level, her share was more. When her son was six months old, her husband, who had become a heroin addict, committed suicide with an overdose. Four years later, her son was killed in an automobile accident. By then, we'd been together for a couple of years and had an infant daughter of our own. In the ongoing months, the changes in our lives were settled into, with a sense of defenselessness. Sex and the lilt of intimacy lacked permission. Moments of happiness were guarded at best. I was too young and too self-involved to believe that we couldn't recover from this. But by the time our son was born, a year-and-a-half later, it was apparent that, with its essential depth unaltered, the limits we faced in our marriage were more or less permanent. One everyday observable quality, which seemed to increase with time, was Elaine's inability to tolerate even the slightest pain. She had no threshold for it, physical or psychological. The pursuit of places in the sun—with the hope of rescuing our marriage—was, on another level, purely a flight from pain. This was perhaps even truer in Elaine's separations

from me. But then, paradoxically, the pain of being alone was something she could elude only by coming back.

After the death of Elaine's son, friends of ours in San Francisco invited us to come out and stay with them for a while. One afternoon, shortly after we arrived, they took us to a group exhibition at the San Francisco Art Institute. I particularly remembered two or three canvases of figures on black-and-white tiled floors, painted with thick paint and fearless energy. This was the first time I saw Joan Brown's work.

A YEAR OR SO after the *Mary Julia* show, Elaine left New Mexico and returned to Canada to live with her parents. The children stayed with me in Santa Fe. They spent their summers with Elaine and, when she moved back to New York, their high school years.

JOAN TOLD ME she had begun the *Mary Julia Series* after finding a large stack of twenty-four- by thirty-six-inch paper abandoned on a loading dock in the Mission District of San Francisco. It was a little like the mythic novel that a ream of blank paper represents to a writer; although in Joan's case, unlike what generally happens with writers, she promptly "filled it in." From early success while she was still an art student, to her death at fifty-two, her work underwent shifts in style and focus. At the same time, it was consistently autobiographical. Whatever one ultimately thinks of it, a whole life is in it. Looked at now, the big-brush, thick impasto paintings of the late fifties and early sixties that established her reputation—*Brambles* (1957), *Bob, Sultana, Guard* (1961), *Eye Trees in the Park in Madrid* (1961)—convey a sense of making, seeing, and talent that has outdistanced the rambunctious impact for which they were initially prized. Her transitional periods are uneven but marked by breakthroughs, like the series of ballroom dancers in the early seventies and the paintings of Charlie Sava, her swimming coach. By 1975

the paint is thin, flat, and hard-edged in pictures like *After the Alcatraz Swim #3*. With stark restraint, they seem to hold their breath. In 1976, with the *Mary Julia Series*, she achieves a brilliant balance between drawing and an active painterly surface. She works with willful candor that continues to renew rather than resolve the terms of her pictures—the last stroke is as fresh as the first and has the same unrehearsed virtue. In this sustained body of work, with its sexy, winsome energy and beguiling impatience toward inessentials, she has made a kind of contemporary ukiyo-e.

It isn't far-fetched to think of 1976 as a high point in Joan's career. The *Mary Julia Series* alone consists of forty-seven pictures. Two other separately numbered series, done that year in the same format—*Mary Julia & David* and *Mary Julia & Nick*—are in effect a continuation of the series. She also completed a series called *David & Stephanie*, and another called *Celeste*, as well as several major paintings, including *Let's Dance*, *The Kiss*, and *The End of the Journey*.

Along with the work of De Forest, Robert Colescott, William T. Wiley, and a few other West Coast artists, Joan's achievement anticipated by a number of years the Neo-Expressionist painters of the eighties in New York. Yet her evolution was less a polemical stance against Minimalism and Conceptual Art, which characterized the New York movement, than it was a personal and persistent exploration, anchored in figurative painting.

A final series, *Mary Julia in Trouble*, was done in 1977. These are gray, gridded drawings, in a perfunctory mood, of a female figure tormented by a life-size rat and a skeleton. As Klimenko explained, "They represent Joan working through a bad time with a boyfriend." By the end of 1977, her work was again in transition and although there were exceptions, usually in the case of self-portraits, her paintings over the next few years—reflecting an interest in Eastern mysticism— grew somewhat stilted. Yet, Matisse, Rembrandt, Velazquez, and Goya were a deep source of her strength as an artist. It's difficult to imagine that, given enough time, their influence wouldn't have prevailed in the ultimate development of her work.

JOAN AND I had dinner a couple of times before she went back to San Francisco. I showed her around Santa Fe, but there were no midnight swims. Under other circumstances there might or might not have been. In any case, we became friends.

JOAN BROWN WAS KILLED, in 1990, in a construction accident in India, where she was installing a tiled obelisk.

IN 1997, Elaine checked into a hospital in Rosarito Beach, Mexico, with terminal melanoma cancer. I was living in New York. We had remained close, connected by the children but also by an indelible bond. Among the various things I sent her—books and so forth—was a *Mary Julia* poster. Art was a part of our lives. We talked on the phone. There were palm trees outside her window.

Mary Julia

WILLIAM BENTON received his early training in music, and worked as a jazz musician before becoming a writer. His poetry has been published in the *New Yorker*, the *Paris Review*, *Open City*, and in several collections. He is the author of *Exchanging Hats*, a book on the paintings of Elizabeth Bishop, and a novel, *Madly*. He lives in New York City.